T0207980

WOMAN OF THE MOON

A compilation of poems
aspiring to describe
the impossible,
attempting to define love.

PAMELA WASABI

BALBOA.PRESS
A DIVISION OF HAY HOUSE

Balboa Press books may be ordered through booksellers or by contacting:

Balboa Press
A Division of Hay House
1663 Liberty Drive
Bloomington, IN 47403
www.balboapress.com
1 (877) 407-4847

Print information available on the last page.

ISBN: 978-1-9822-3995-4 (sc)
ISBN: 978-1-9822-3996-1 (e)

Balboa Press rev. date: 01/09/2020

To my Lover.

Whom I've loved in many faces,
Through whom I've reached the Divine.

CONTENTS

Woman of The Moon: A compilation of poems aspiring to describe the impossible, attempting to define love.

SACRED
HELLOO

Dear Reader,

Thank you for picking up my book.
In your hands, you hold an open heart.
A heart like yours, made of paper and ink.
A heart that pumps stories, tears, and joy.

A heart that has seen beauty, inexplicable beauty.
A heart that has loved.
A heart that has suffered.

Alan Watts said poetry is the art of saying what can't be said
with words.
Writing is the medium through which I breathe,
and poetry the way in which my heart aspires to define the
unexplainable: love.

I've been captivated by the concept of pain.
All my life, like any of us, I've wanted to understand the reason
behind our misery.
This book put itself together to answer that question.
It's not suffering or pain that we should wonder about.
It's not pain that makes us do things or say things.
It's love.

The presence of love is like warm honey pouring over our
shoulders.
It's like the kissing away of a Miami Sunset.
Love is the only universal truth understood by every living
being,
from the tiniest of the fleas on my cat's black tail, looking to
propagate life,
to a majestic sun seeking to court the moon on a silver sky.
Love binds with blinding purpose.

But it's feeling undeserving of love that confuses us,
making us feel like there's no horizon, no hope.
But love never ceases to exist.
It's our scared selves who shy away from accepting the gift of
existence that resides in us.
Love is powerful, and that can be intimidating.
We are made *of* love.
Love is us.

Throughout this book, I narrate different phases of life broken
down into different poems —attempting to describe love.
Each one of them is the light that a relationship, an encounter,
a heartbreak, a waking-up moment left behind.

It's the essence of what makes us human.
It's falling in love and falling apart.
It's giving birth, being kind, or feeling ferocious.
It's being confused and being sad.
It's the light that illuminates our way to find beauty in every
single dark sky of our lives.

It's love.

A love that I can't singularly define because love is everything.

SACRED LIFE

What stories do you need to tell yourself
to justify choosing you first?

The word "Love" doesn't do justice to what Love really is.
Between those four letters stories, encounters, tears, and
joy reside.
It's in our cynical, manic, compulsive way of trying to label
it all that we've fallen victim to our own game.
We forget what it is, thus Love is undefinable.

To define Love is like putting a leash on a feral animal.
Love is not from our three-dimensional reality.
Love is an ever-changing wave of electricity.
Love hurts like a beast scraping down your chest and
chewing on your heart.
And Love is the understanding to forgive that.

Love has a thousand and one hats.
Love is many things and is no-thing.
Yet, Love is the little things.
Love is the verb of teaching, listening, empathizing...
sharing.
Love is intense. It's strength.
Love is the mere action of saying hello to a forgotten
friend.
It's the untouchable force behind a smile.

To Love is to be.
I Love you, lover of the past, and present, and future.
I Love you, friend, and I Love you, stranger.
I Love you, universe.

Love is eternal

Love can't be described, you live it.
Love can't be explained, you feel it.
Love can't be measured, you transmit it.

Say I Love you more often.
It's harmless, but its rippling embracing effect is eternal.

Nothing is.
And everything is.
Take a look at the world again.
When I say it's beautiful,
And you say it' fucked up,
None of us hold the truth.
Life is not beautiful or fucked up.
Life is not masculine or feminine.
Life is not a yes or a no.
Life is not right or wrong.
Life is not ambiguous.
Life is.

Life happens.
Life propagates.
Life flows in spite of our human commentary.
Life exists.
Life is.

And that "is" —
is the most fucking beautiful statement
that has ever been.

Love is life

We are inspired by someone else's story.
We fight to defend a story we believe in.

Growing up, we are told stories of the world.
Growing up, we are convinced of stories to shape our
behavior;
to eat our food, to not talk to strangers and to be a good
human.

We go to sleep with a bedtime story.

We explain the world through stories.
We share stories.
We tell stories.
We laugh, we cry to stories.
We pay to see a story.
We argue about stories.
We make choices based on our own story.
We learn stories, and we teach those stories.
We forget stories.

If every author of every story is also telling a story he once
was told —
If everyone, every culture, every being, every mind tells a
story that gives meaning to its life...who holds the truth?

Our life is but a story we love to tell.

Love is a good story

Gotta stop dreaming of what's not here. Gotta stop longing for what you don't have. Dreaming or longing for something are not affirmations. The only thing you are affirming is the fact that you don't have what you want. You gotta sink into your skin and observe from a distance—you. You gotta stop identifying yourself with the circumstances. This "right-now" is not who you are. That "over-there" is not who you are. You are the choice of how you choose to see yourself today.

You are infinite possibilities.

Love is infinite possibilities

I committed myself to ask to be used by the greater power for the greater good. I just happened to oversee the small font at the end of this imaginary deal I made with life.

It reads the following:
You will be used for greatness.
You will be a messenger of truth.
You will be seen as a mirror.

Then, these were printed in tiny font:

You will be put in embarrassing circumstances and unbearable situations — for the greater good.
You will undergo moments of sorrow and heartaches — in search of the truth.
You will be put through the most challenging relationships — for the greater good.
You will find yourself in those you can't resist, can't stand and can't understand — in search of the truth.

You will be used as an example of truth capable of change.

You will change the collective understanding that pain is a matter of perception, that agony doesn't need to linger, that suffering is an illusion—

Now that I know this,
I still ask to be used for the greater good in search of the truth.

A hibiscus flower.
A wave.
The "Super Moon."
A cat with six toes.
A Hemingway in love.
A cool breezy night.
A violet sky.
A flamingo feather.
Street straw art.
An acrobat with no audience.
A Russian man selling corn.
A red sun.
A coral house.

Are all expressions of love.

I see myself in all of it.
In the Russian man, in the moon, in the red sun, in all.
I've felt someone watching,
Even when there was no audience.
Or no one buying corn.

We walk around this Earth trying making sense of our
existence.
We are spread out like branches and roots of one same tree.
We embrace the world,
providing shade, or corn, or fire, or a show.

All expressions of love.

Love is an expression

I see it all, in all.
All of us a reflection of each other.
Trying to make sense of life,
Expressing our love.

—

Notes from a trip to Key West, 2019

I love my ex.
But not in a romantic way.
I brotherly love him.
Once you love, how can you unlove?

You can't.
Sometimes we have sex
Out of the familiarity of knowing each other's bodies,
Out of the necessity to fill each other's void.
We know what tickles our exhales.
We know how to position our fingers.
We know how to love each other's loneliness.
But we aren't each other's partner.
But we are each other's trigger.

One wrong word that slips from his mouth and I shoot
artillery out of my throat.
One wrong move, the wrong tone,
His whistling when I need to concentrate,
His stubbornness,
His inexplicable way of being right when I'm wrong
The pointing of his finger into my fresh wounds—
Makes me want to not love him,
Never to have met him,
Makes me want to not see him or know his name.
But I can't unlove him.

But I can evolve from that love.
In seeing the man in his eyes and not my rival.
In talking to him as a person and not my opponent.
In understanding he is my teacher and the toughest,

Love is to evolve

who's showing me the shadowed aspects of myself I need to
work on,
so I can heal them, and then I can move on.
Who's shining a mirror from his chest, reflecting my stubborn
ways showing me what pisses me off the most about myself.

Love has a weird way of asking the best of you.
You can't unlove, but you can evolve.
In loving him as a human, a brother after all.

I live for the day when we remember we are human.
I live for the day when we forget about perfection.
For being human is being fragile, like the leftover ashes
from an incense stick after burning.
For being human is being flawed, like the cracks on a
Japanese vase that's later filled with gold,
like a loose thread at the end of the sweater sleeve you like
to chew on,
like an ugly tomato— so juicy,
like the phone ringing and it being an unexpected person.
But isn't that a sort of perfection?

Take the clothes off.
Find your pod.
Melt with your bones and the blood and your thoughts.
Forget how to speak.
Stare at our heart.
Disintegrate at the drop of your tears.
Become a solution.
Liberate the soul.
And know that from this place of oneness, of dissolved being,
you can perceive the humanity of it all,
where things break, melt, burn, and become undone.

Know that every death brings beauty forward.
Like the caterpillar that boils in the chrysalis before
becoming the butterfly.
Like the fetus in the darkness before seeing light.

I live for the day when you accept your humanity as just
perfect.

Love is human

15

Probably the biggest mistake we can make as parents
is to sell our children the idea of love as a possession.

It's probably the biggest and stupidest lie we live every day
as a society,
defining love as loving someone and expecting something
in return.

Expecting to be saved, to be seen, to be rescued, to be talked
to in exchange for your love it's ransom. It's to say you give
your hugs and your kisses and your kindness in exchange of
a kind of life insurance — Like to pay for friends to come to
your funeral. Like to strategically placed your loved ones in
your chess game, so if you lose, there's someone to blame.
It's to ask people to love you first.
It's to say to your kid that you can only love him if he
cleans his plate.

No, love cannot be conditional.

Love can not be selective.
Love is like spiked water —it's feral.
It inebriates what it touches.
It dampens with fervor.
Love needs to be set free.
Love is to be given.
Unconditionally.

Daughter of mine, I know I've done well when I see you
setting yourself free
from our conditioned and limited ways of understanding love.

Love is unconditional

Never dreamed of having children.
But it happened as a divine accident.
I was crowned a mother by her existence.
And now I feel privileged to be committed to her love.
My little piece of violet heavens, my miracle, my blood, my
extension.

I'm young, and troubled... a wonderer.

I don't have many answers, and I'm wrong many times.
But tucking this delicate soul in bed every night and
waking up to her a little bit older, grounds me.

It's impossible to understand her perfection.
She's pure, and precious, and my daughter but not my
possession.
I just protect her and provide for her.
And with her innocent few years of existence
she's the one teaching me about life.

A moment of clarity,
when you feel like life makes sense.
It's like feeling your spirit has weight over your body.
Just like air lifts a gas balloon into the sky.
A moment of clarity is knowing your every breath makes a
difference.
It's feeling the unachievable can be conquered by the
knights of your soul.

A moment of clarity can be found in the steam arising
from a couple in love.
In watching an Olympic athlete spin on ice like a
hypnotizing force.
A moment of clarity is a runner's high.

A moment of clarity is understanding your purpose.
It's the force that propels your creativity to find solutions,
to find shiny needles in a stack of dull hay.

A moment of clarity is blinding light.
It's to see with your peripheral vision.
It's to see with your hands, and your skin,
and your guts and your heart.

A moment of clarity is inspiration,
which can only be felt when you believe what you see is the
manifestation of your dreams.
A moment of clarity is the sign you've been waiting for.
A moment of clarity is when you believe you can.
And if you do, you will flow through life like the shaking
hips of a Lebanese belly dancer.

Love is a moment of clarity

Has it ever occurred to you, that what you have learned to
define as love could be an illusion?

Mom didn't know better.
She grew in a Machiavellic world,
Where love was taught through fear.
She learned love was not free,
She had to work for it.
She had to deserve it.

Dad left home at an early age seeking sanity.
He thought love was the absence of violence.
He never knew what a kiss on the cheek meant.
He learned love was for other people.
He felt he didn't belong.

Grandma was taught never to speak.
Grandpa learned never to cry.

Great-Grandma was told who to marry.
Great-Grandpa learned not to question authority.

Great-Great-Grandma was burnt at the stake.
Great-Great-Grandpa learned he was born a sinner.

Our ancestor's innocence was stolen,
Like clipping the wings from a bird.
They didn't get to fly,
They couldn't imagine what that was.
But they felt it in a dream.
In that dream, they saw a younger side of themselves,

Love is to fly

Soaring through the skies, racing with eagles; touching
freedom.
They were trying to speak to you, and they said:

Spread your wings,
Leave the cage,
Trust yourself,
Speak freely.

Experience love by your own means.
Love is free. Love is you.
We might have not known how to teach you this love,
But that doesn't mean you cannot know it.

You don't need permission to fly.

The ocean gushed all over me today.
How many melodies are sung when she caresses the shore.
She carries the oxygen I breathe.

She told me she loves me.
She called me her lover.
She gave me all of herself.
My beloved ocean.

I told her,

I love to play among your turquoise sheets.
But I have nothing to offer you in return to match your
gifts and your greatness.

She said,

Giving and receiving are one in truth[1]
She told me to embrace what I receive.

That when I do, I'll be able to —
To gush all over my lover, and all over my world,
To share my love for life and my adoration for living.

Giving and receiving are one in truth.

Love is the ocean

---

[1] Course in Miracles, Lesson 108

In my low days, love is but a mere attraction that never feels quite the same.
It transforms; it never stays the same.

In my high days, love is but energy that transforms me; and I'll never be the same.

God is oftentimes found in human form.
Like when you love someone.
Like when you love yourself.
Like when love happens.
Like when love is.

Like when you experience compassion,
and forgiveness,
and sweetness,
and grace.

God is oftentimes found in human form.

Love is god

SACRED UNION

The truth that resides in your heart is my favorite love story.

Love is the sustenance of existence. Even atoms, at
the quantic level, are romantic particles that stand at a
distance from each other, and only an inexplicable force
keeps them bonded forever. Some call that force energy,
or the electromagnetic field. It could also be called love.
Love is essential. It's the current that brings two beings,
under the magnetism of that energetic force, into a
relationship. Love is chemistry. Love is the union of two
aware and actualized souls that commit to growing with
each other, through each other and for each other. Love
is compatibility. Love is relatable. Love is when one loves
oneself with such vastness and fury that love itself exudes
from one's pores. Love then floods with such compulsion
that it envelops everything it sees. Love is communication.
Love is the expression of one's life wanting to be shared
with another romantic.

I know you because I love you.
Or, I love you because I know you.
Or, loving you is to know you?
Or, knowing you is to love you.

Not sure what happened first,
but know this,
I love you because I love myself.

Love is knowing you

I fall in love with sensitive people.

They tell their story in some sort of artistic way: with the way they walk with wings hanging from their scapula, with the way they keep their shoulders back and hearts open, with the way they finish their sentences with a smirk or a smile, with the way they tie their hair up and sip black coffee.

Their stories are not always pretty, but their sensitivity in telling them is beautiful.

I fall in love with sensitive people.

They make the ugly inspiring.
They make struggles worthy of longing.
They make life far more interesting.
They see what's not shown.
They see behind what's in front.
They have 20/20 vision into the unknown.

Sensitive people find beauty in the minuscule:
In one of my freckles.
In the length of my pinkie.
In the taste of my dimple.
In the smell of my armpit.
In my unbalanced nipples.

And so, I fall in love over and over again with them, even though they can easily fall in love, even with pain. They romanticize it, they justify it.

Love is sensitive

I'm a sensitive person also.
I find beauty in their struggle
—which becomes my struggle too,
loving someone who's in love with suffering.

I don't "love" you; I "pain" you.
I don't understand you; I feel you.
I don't see you; I taste you.
I empathize with you.

I can't "love" you.
I can only see in you what I recognize in myself.
We are both in pain.

I want to love you.
I "pain" to be with you.

They're so close, love from pain.

Love is scary

I crawled into bed. He was expecting me.
I got up on my knees. He met me.
I stared at his eyes. He placed his hands on my shoulders.
I stayed still. He flicked my satin straps down.
He undressed me.
Not only was my nudity now uncovered.
He unzipped his way to my heart.

Love is naked

No. It was not "in love" what I wanted to say.
I'm not "in love" I am "in one."
It's the feeling of completeness, of wholeness.
But a wholeness with no bottom, an all-ness.

I'm in one with you.
I'm falling in all.

I love out of my own selfishness.
I desire to love, I require to love.
To keep this heart beating
I must give. By giving may I go on living.

In giving I find my Wild Woman.
In giving I find my love.
In loving is my joie de vivre.
In loving I am the Universe.
In loving my self dissolves
creative power overflows.
With that power
I write books, I write poems.
I make passion fruit pies
and lavender cookies.
I jump from airplanes,
I swim with sharks.

When I love like I only know how,
when I pour myself unapologetically,
when I give myself abundantly;
I'm fearless.

And because of that
I love unconditionally,
out of my own selfishness.

Love is powerful

I'm the tallest mountain.
I'm the strongest rock.
I'm the deepest ocean.
You can climb on me.
You can lean on me.
You can dive in me.
I don't break.

The question is:
Can you deal with my immensity?

Love is the storm

Don't you know that I have scales for skin?
I swim better than I talk.
I can take a storm.
I'm made of salt water.
Here, taste my tears; lick my sweat.
I can take any storm.

To see the rain is to see my soul.
To see your storm is a firework show.
I watch in awe.
I see your scars and your broken bones.
I don't judge.

I'll be the ocean to receive you when you fall.

I see your pain, I have a space for it.
Under my waves and my curves.

I just *wanna* love you.
If it takes for me to be the fish, or the ocean, or the waves,
I'll change forms.
Just like the water— I've heard that's why liquid is called a
solution.

I have so much to hydrate your dry heart.
So much wildernesses to keep you busy at my shore.
So much sweetness to feed you with my foam.

I can take your storm.

Love is visceral

I'm finally falling in love with myself.
And it's because of that love that I can love you.
I love you tangibly with my guts.

It's an addiction. It's the oxygen I need.
If my love is deprived,
I have to taste the lips of a glass and
the pouring of grape history down my throat.
I have to kiss my cigar and exhale its aroma after it has
made love to me.
I have to touch myself and remind me that I am enough.
I am all I need.
And that I can love you because I love myself.

I can't love you exclusively.
I love every something.
I love the everything.
To love is my natural state.
I love, just like I breathe and just like I am.
I love you as I love the ocean, as I love a bird chirping in
my window.
I love you as I love existing.

I love myself so fiercely that I can love you viscerally.

SACRED
SEX
UALITY

Love is not from this world, love created this world.

Don't judge a snake because she wiggles on the ground.
Or because she sizzles when she sees you.
She carries the kind of wisdom only an armless and legless
animal can understand.
She was not condemned to lack extremities, she was gifted
a privilege.
She's closer to the Earth's heart — she keeps its secrets.
She has a unique perspective.
She's grounded like no other.
But she's been banned, and booed, and deemed ugly.
When in fact, she is a powerful creature.
A dangerous one.

Because

She represents feminine wisdom.
She represents liberation from the ego.
She represents sexual awareness.

Funny how such a beautiful creature becomes a burden to
our society.
Perhaps we live scared of our own potential,
of all that that invites us to uncoil.

Bite the apple!

Love is kundalini

Meet her.
She resides in your root chakra.
She's Kundalini energy.
When she wakes up,
Your snake-like spine becomes a bridge between the ground and
the Divine.

Next time you gotta tell somebody to "fuck off," do a favor to the world, and tell them to "go masturbate." We can appease the rigidity of the world by having more orgasms when going to bed, and less bitterness when going to sleep.

Love is an orgasm

Unleash your wild beast, beauty.
Caress yourself like you appreciate every pore of your living
body.
Do it slowly, to the tempo of the rain outside your window.
Wake up every neuron, and every space between every
atom.

Squeeze your thighs and your butt chicks with your bare
hands,
and release with your every exhale an "I love you."

Swim with your hands around your waist, and your
tummy, and your scars.

Grab your breasts and thank them for their beauty,
for how they defy gravity,
for how they sit like the Queen's Guards protecting your
heart.

Hug your neck with your fingers.
Stay there for a bit, trace the kisses that have been
and make room for the ones that will be.

Stroll your hand through your maine.
Mess it up.
Exhale, howl, roar.
Keep breathing.

Love is playful

You are making love to yourself but you are not alone.
The universe is breathing you.
It is kissing you.
When you play with yourself,
You are making love to the universe.

My pussy wants to cry.

When it cries
my eyes become so jealous
they shut off and turn inwards to stare at my guts
to experience the rain and the release.

That sweet and tender part of my thighs
the one you like to bite,
the one that surrounds my Flower tingles,
anxiously awaiting the downpour.
I feel as if bugs are crawling over my torso.
Waves of energy amuse my every cell
from the tips of my toes to the crown of my head.

My whole body becomes a rainforest,
with the smell of musk
and the sound of waterfalls.

My legs fold open like butterflies.
My hips— if they have paint on their edges
will trace the most beautiful flowers
with their circular, repetitive motion.
This is how they talk.
This is how they accept.
This is how they say yes.

But why does my pussy want to cry?
Because when I love my life-birthing ecosystem,
When I recognize my creative-making potential,
it is too damn beautiful not to cry.

When my pussy cries I give birth to myself,
And it cries because
It's the cry of joy;
it's the cry of Love.

When the Divine Masculine speaks, I listen.
I surrender, I submit.
I also do other things on my knees.

Woman of The Moon

Lover,

Relax your mind.
If there are thoughts that start pulling you out of this
moment,
pretend they are clouds in your mind.
Watch them pass through your sky.

I'm traveling with my awareness of where I am in my
room,
to be around you, across distances, in your bed.

Now, I'm in your room,
coming through the gap of your blinds as blue sun rays.
I'm in your walls. I'm in your bedsheets. I'm in the air that
surrounds you.

I take form.
You can't touch me,
but you can feel my sensation as a cool breeze over you.
I'm getting acquainted with your skin and your pores,
and as you relax deeper,
my form turns into this aqua shadow
that sits at the end of the bed, at your feet.

I take your left foot between my hands and massage it
gently.
I then kiss your toe. You moan a little.
I take that as consent to seduce you.

I start climbing up your body.
My lips are at your knees.

I'm on my fours.
My pussy drips a little on your leg.
I keep moving.
I start my ascent toward your heart.
I kiss my way up your dick.
He's laying there. Not aroused yet.

Your mind hasn't relaxed, although it wants to.
But there's a force that you have no control of called gravity
that starts pulling your worry, your stress, your fears down your
cock.
Like a magnet.

I'm there. Licking the tip of your dick.
Just inserting it in my mouth, so delicately.
And as I do it, the clouds evaporate from your sky,
and a beautiful orange and purple dawn now colors your mind.

Your dick has changed temperature.
It's warm, and it wants to give itself to my mouth.
I take it in my hands and insert it all the way down my throat.
It starts erecting within me.
And as I caress your dick up and down with my whole mouth,
I pull all your thoughts for once out of you.
Don't worry.
I'm not gonna carry your stress.
It evaporates when out of your localized awareness.

I hear you moaning. It's a short one.
You close your eyes. And your sky turns black as night.
I'm wet. And I feel a tingling in my pussy.

It's that feeling of wanting to devour you.
But I wait. I breathe.

Your dick is now hard.
I continue my rise up your stomach, your ribs.
I make a pit stop at your right nipple. My tongue plays with it.
And now, every time you moan, you shoot stars across your
mind —your dark sky.

I extend your arms wide open.
I'm now laying on top of you.
My arms over yours, my hands in yours, and we lace together
our fingers.
My pussy and your dick naturally want to consume each other,
interlock each other.

I kiss your neck on your left side.
This time you are not shy about your desire for me.
You moan louder now, letting loose more stars into the
darkness.
I take your hands and bring them closer to your head,
and at the same time let your dick penetrate me all the way deep
inside.

You are inside of me, but my awareness has transcended your
skin.
I'm inside of you, and we are sharing the same starry night sky.
I keep kissing your neck.
I feel your heart changing beats.
I can hear its rhythm.
I use it as the music I snake dance to, on top of you.

You turn your head to find my lips.
We stare at each other for a bit.
A tenth of a second that seems an eternity.
It's a fraction of a second that's always available to us.
It's how we call upon each other, and no matter the distance, we
can find us in that instant...

In that reality there's steam.
Our bodies are doing what they know to do to know each other
better.
They rock each other.
Our souls find peace between the vibrational convulsion.
Our collapsed awareness relaxes,
as if it was laying back on a grassy field looking up at the
immensity of the sky.

We kiss. We come.
And we shoot a blinding Sun.

The future is feline.

The future is not feminine as a secluded notion that steps on top of the masculine, proposing division, proliferating duality and a never-ending battle of the sexes.

The feminine must rise from her intuitive-feline, daring, sensual and curious innate power. She must rise from her transformative and healing ability, and recognize her magical gift of life-giver to all things, projects and solutions. She must be fierce like a lioness, and act from a deep sense of responsibility, tending to her life, children and her home.

The future is feline.

The future belongs to our kids. The future belongs to an equalitarian society where the Sacred Feminine is cherished and the Masculine is respected. The future is feline for men, too.

The masculine must step down from its fear-driven, material-accumulative approach through which he measures success. The feminine awaits for the masculine to rise in his kingship archetype of a lion.
The masculine must live up to his role as king and provide protection of all life and all life-bearing creatures. He should honor the governing rules of the universe: all creatures are created equal.
He must pull up his strength and his courage to defeat the ego-mind that's endangering our world.

Love is feline

The King of the Jungle is a man who knows his mission and purpose in life.
He measures his strength by the vastness of his wisdom and with his actions, provided they are acts of respect and honor that contribute to the beauty and evolution of our Sacred Earth.

The Divine Masculine is a man of his roar.
His word is righteousness.
And he adores the Wild Woman.

The future is feline because our Nature-giving power is our intuition.
That power lives in all sentient and non-sentient beings in the universe—as it is the information downloaded directly from the Source.

In such a world, which is the potential of ours, the feminine is no lesser or supreme or separated from the masculine. In such a Sacred Universe, the masculine and the feminine present themselves as inseparable and complementing, presenting a new entity with their Sacred Union.

When the feminine and masculine come together as one, they give birth to the world.

The future is feline.

Love is not attachment.
Love is not forced.
Love is not imposed by limits.
Love is not when in doubt.
Love is not when expecting.
Love is not when judgement abides.
Love is not a strategic act.
Love is not a game where there's a winner.
Love is not control.
Love is not linear.

Sex is not attachment.
Sex is not forced.
Sex is not imposed by limits.
Sex is not when in doubt.
Sex is not when expecting.
Sex is not when judgement abides.
Sex is not a strategic act.
Sex is not a game where there's a winner.
Sex is not control.
Sex is not linear.

Love listens.
Love is transparent.
Love is open.
Love is patient.
Love is acceptance.
Love is surrender.

Love is sex

Sex listens.
Sex is transparent.
Sex is open.
Sex is patient.
Sex is acceptance.
Sex is surrender.

Is love sex?

SACRED HEALING

Enlightenment is the technological
advancement of the human mind.

To remain in fear is as ironic as wanting to keep your eyes closed in the dark because you can't see anything. But if you open your eyes, you will become acquainted with the darkness. Blackness will become your friend, a known territory. A place where the only ones that survive are those who stare fear in the eyes.

Love is to wake up

"What do I want?" he asked me.

I've read relationship books that praise that question as a
very smart one,
because it means the man sees the woman.
But I've also read in my eastern gurus and my Taoist
philosophers,
that that's an unquestionable question.
Because one, you already have what you want.
And two, you are not done getting to know yourself to
know what you want.

"What do I want?" It's a question with its own storyline.
It has a beginning by breakfast,
a cusp by lunch and by dinner,
it's a completely different poem.

What do I want? I want to be me.
What do I want if I'm a book in progress?
I want to act from love, and not from fear.

Does that answer your question?
Can you see me?

But what good is the answer if you can't give me, me.
Shouldn't the question be,
what do you want?

And after discussing Alan Watts,
you know the answer is somewhat to be you...

Is there, in you, space for me?

In being me, there's space for love.

So if, with your original question,
you attempted to see me because you wanted to meet me.
Can you meet me as the love I make space for?

And if my answer puzzles you.
If I turned your question into a riddle,

Can't you see, that all a woman wants, is to love?

We have all experienced heartbreak.
We are familiar with that feeling when that person is not
here anymore.
Whether they passed away.
Whether they left.

Heartbreak is as close as feeling incomplete.
Like getting out of bed and a piece of us stays buried
underneath the pillows.
It's feeling like the ground doesn't extend past our
bedroom.
Like feeling vertigo before taking the next step.

But there's another type of heartbreak.
Pain still overpowers existence.
But the choice taken that caused heartbreak,
Was not caused by the leaving of someone.
But by choosing you first.

Choosing you first is not commonly applauded.
But it means choosing your freedom.
This choice causes pain because you have to detach
yourself from someone, or something, or an idea.

And when that happens,
Pain, and sorrow override your soul.
You feel complete and it's overwhelming.

Love is freedom

Pamela Wasabi

But it's a heartache caused by the liberation of what you thought
you were
Into that you know you are.
Freedom has an aching price.
It comes from heart-breaking the mold,
And choosing you first.

—

#plannedparenthood

Compassion is to see God even in the darkest places.
Like, in my heart when you left.
Like, in your heart when you felt unworthy of me.

I have a wild imagination.
I try to read destiny's future.

I have a wild imagination.
I looked at you and saw so much more.
I saw strength, confidence, space for me.

I have a wild imagination.
I saw things I wanted to see.

Now that you are gone, I daydream.
I bring the past to my tomorrow.
I picture the laughter, the hugs,
the clothes over the floor mapping a road to the bed.
I think of you and me.

I have a wild imagination.
I want to get to the part when you become history.
I want my present free of sorrows.

Wild imagination, would you give me a hand?

But, wait!

If I believe what I imagine, is that me creating my reality
or entering the domain of insanity?

If I still dream of you —am I a lunatic?

Love is my imagination

Mind: What's are these feelings?
Heart: A feeling is the child of your imagination; a mere interpretation.
Mind: Of what?
Heart: Of what you think your relationship was.
Mind: About what happened?
Heart: About how you perceived it.
Mind: So was it real, or a product of my imagination?
Heart: Your reality is a projection of your imagination.
Mind: But did it happen? Was it love?
Heart: Were you expecting something in return?
Mind: Yes.
Heart: Then, no.

Heart: Seek the truth that is found in the purpose.
Mind: Isn't the purpose the desired feeling that comes with a relationship?
Heart: No. Feelings are barometers of the truth. They are not the truth. Just like the fact that the clock reads 7:47 p.m. right now does not define time. Whatever feelings you seek others to fulfill in you, as if this is the result you are expecting, are the emotions you are neglecting to give to your own self.
You are just placing your responsibility of self-fulfillment outside of you.

Heart: Is your motivation of being in a relationship driven by the outcome?
Mind: Yes. Isn't that the way it goes?
Heart: You can't have expectations in a relationship.
Mind: So what's the purpose?
Heart: To dance. Be the giver. Love unconditionally.
Be the receiver embrace the music. Dance!

You broke me open.
For that, I'm grateful to you forever.
I shattered, and when I collected all my pieces,
I put myself together in a way that when light hits me,
I reflect rainbows like the prism of a crystal.

I thought I was made of glass.
After giving you my heart and getting it stabbed,
I realized I'm too much for your cold coven,
I'm too precious to be kept in the dark,
I need to shine, I am light.
I'm precious like a quartz.

Love is light

When a heart breaks, love spills out...
—

He reached out to me that night.
I was already lying in bed.
He texted me.
We started chatting, and his words touched me in all the
right places.
His were those texts that when you receive them,
you close your eyes and imagine feeling so light that you
have to grab onto the sheets or the bedframe to keep from
flying out the window.
He was sweet.
He didn't speak of the things he wanted to do to me.
He spoke of how he saw me —he knows me, he gets me.
He held me in between the silence of my phone vibrating
and those three dots on the screen announcing more of his
poetic courting.

He came over that night.
We didn't say much.
We hugged, we kissed, we undressed.
We felt each other in each other.
He smelled my love spilling over.
He read in my eyes what my heart held and couldn't hide.
He embraced me. I got lost in his beard.
His chest kept me warm, and I found a place to rest my
head.

Love is spilling over

We didn't talk much that night.
But he picked up the broken pieces of my heart and loved them back together.

He saw me.

In my love path, I've dated some beautiful men.
In my opinion, each showed me a facet of the Divine
Masculine.
The problem was, little did they know of their own
Divinity.
Most of them walked away with the same story.
They couldn't be emotionally available to me.
Every single relationship, every single encounter, is a
mirror through which partners observe each other.
We can observe in our reflection the hidden wounds that
being alone dimmed.
To have encountered men closing their hearts, meant mine
was closed too, so I've worked on opening my heart, and
kept it open.
I've worked on facing my fears that were highlighted in my
partner's reflection.
I've worked on staying through the most tumultuous
situations—instead of running away—to learn what I
needed to learn.
I've been sad and upset at them, but have found a place to
offer them my compassion.
However, after looking at the same image over and over
again, and gone through my healing, I realized that this
mirror might also be pushing me back to make some
reflections.
What I see now in these very sensitive men are confused
and unclear minds.
Men that keep wandering the earth with a feeling of guilt
that they cannot set aside.
A guilt that is not their own.
They empathize with collective guilt; they feel unworthy,
punishable.

Love is him

They question themselves and their sanity, and they feel
incapable of staying with their partners and looking at their
reflections up close.
These men feel unlovable, and when a woman loves them, they
shun this love and the possibility it could ever truly happen.
They feel incapable of receiving.
How I wish I could show them life through a Wild Woman's
eyes.
I would show them that women don't need men, but we desire
to love them and embrace them.
That we don't expect them to be this or to do that more than
we wish to jump in and love their open hearts.
That all we want is a partner who wishes to explore all the
remote corners of this exciting world, and of the self, while
holding our hand.
I've become a hopeless romantic, a wild poetess, a devotee to a
love that's never conceived.
This love that I have tasted was only incubated in the universe's
womb but never birthed.

Divine Masculine, you don't have to do this alone.
At the end of the birthing canal, there's light and joy and life.
Let's give birth to one another.

The beauty you see in me is your reflection.

We don't love you for what you can provide, we love you for
who you are.
We love you for your ability to face challenges with an open
heart.
We love you for your vulnerability when reaching for help and
holding our hand.

We love you for the warm love that emanates from your being
when you decide --scared shitless, to meet us, feeling nervous
but with a ravenous excitement to make love to life and then
land fully present here with us.

As a woman meeting these men, I don't know what to do.
But, I know what not to do.
I won't hold men in contempt.
And
I won't stop loving them.

We can't survive without water,
and we can't survive without emotional support.

Water is scarce.
Our emotional support lacks.

We will die of sorrow before we die of thirst.
For emotional support is the fountain to which we come
to cry.
It's the shoulder that collects our tears.
It's the ocean that calms our hearts.
It's the river that cleans our wounds.

Without emotional support,
there's no container for all the water we must squeeze out
of our eyes.

And without water, there's no life.

Love is support

If you asked me if I had the chance to go through that
again, would I?
And, if so, would I change anything?
No, I'd say. I wouldn't change a thing, a hair or a beat.
I want to live the calm before the storm.
I want to feel the ocean breeze before I went numb.
I want to have my adventurous heart that now knows
better because it experienced it all.
I wouldn't change a wink.
But... what if I could have loved myself a little bit more?

Wouldn't that change everything?

Love is a little bit more

After a breakup we experience a process of transformation
that carry us from sadness into strength.
It's said to be called mourning; I call it Beautiful Pain.

Walking on that road only our silence can guide us.
It will tell us to be patient and that everything will be ok.
We might know that, but we don't know nothing else.
And is that nothingness that will allow us to find clarity.
Clarity to feel compassion for oneself,
to celebrate the love we once made.
To accept the today and let it hold our hand.
To be thankful for the experiences that fed us in the past.
When you thank this beautiful pain, you will start to shed.

Shake off of all the dry skin, heavy traumas and thorns of
the past.
Cherish this delicate moment.
You are experiencing a transformation,
growing new buds,
plantings more seeds,
calling in new bees.
You are strong,
you've loved,
you've grown and you are ready to live more.

I didn't know what I was doing.
I knew I was writing, but I didn't know what I was doing.
I was confessing my love to the paper.
I was trusting all I had in me to the pen.
I wrote without looking back.
I wrote forward.
I wrote my way out of myself.

I let my hand lead me.
She'd find traces and footprints of letters that seemed to
have been here before.
I didn't even want to look.
Sometimes, she wrote faster than my thoughts.
She'd beat an idea being birthed before it had bestowed
upon me.
Before I could feel it.

I didn't know what I was doing, but my body did.
It knew what I was doing as I wrote —
I was talking to my soul.
I was revealing to my heart.
I was healing.

When I write, I come out of myself.
My hand translates what my heart wants to say.
My body knows that when I write, I heal.

I was driving down the Rickenbacker Causeway
and I witnessed a love affair.
I had the sun, posing to my far left in the west
as I drove north over and up the bridge.
He wore an orange smile.
I felt as if he was flirting with me,
but I realized he was looking past me.

His stare was profound, warm,
and it completely transversed me.
He was staring at the moon.
She was in the far east.
She was full.
The Snow Moon.
Wearing her glimmered silver rags.
She was lost in her dreams and in her songs.
She danced and frolicked around the stars
and the different purple shades of the sky.

I felt the passion of the sun.
I felt his desire to cross over the ocean that separated them.
He was in awe of her. He was blushing; turning red.
He knew he couldn't approach her, touch her or smell her.
For the closer he'd come, the farther she'd spin away.

He wondered if she thought of him.
Little did he know,
her inner glow,
her sparkly skin was alive because of him.

The sun had his last minutes counted.
It was time to go away.
Time to meet his fate.
The setting of himself.

He only knew to rise, and lived oblivious of the concept of a
tomorrow.
He only knew about his present.
He only knew about his love.
This love that powered the fervor and ferocity of his splendor.
But he also knew his death was near.
As he set, as he slid down the horizon and disappeared,
he left his last words in majestic pinks, reds and orange-tinted
clouds.
He wrote he was dying happy because he had loved.

I kept driving down the bridge.
The sun's last sigh took over my skin.
Every pore of mine was in love with his love.

And I wondered

If the sun had known about the existence of a tomorrow,
would he have loved the same way?

I look forward to falling in love again,
like the sun,
after many sunsets,
with no tomorrows.

My past relationships failed, but succeeded.
They led me to a path I didn't know existed.

Love always find its way.
Truth is always at my core.

And I'll be dragged
through many *hims*,
and many *hers,*
Till I can come undone.

Love is relationships

SACRED FEMININE

Everyone should be a woman at least once in their many lives.

To be a woman.
To lose your virginity at thirteen.
To have the girls at school point fingers at you.
To be misunderstood.
To be raped at fifteen.
To have to go alone to an abortion clinic.
To feel ashamed.
To have been fingered at two years old when your uncle
was changing your diaper.
To feel like something was stolen from you for the rest of
your life.
To feel disrespected.
To be a virgin and curse it.
To be sold to your husband.
To only feel like you are something when you belong to
someone.
To have your name changed.
To feel valued only if you've kept your legs closed.
To know they can stone you to death otherwise.
To have been burned at the stake.
To have your clit amputated.
To be told not to speak.
To feel unworthy.
To be looked at as if you don't belong in the room.
To be made to feel invisible.
To be paid less than your male peers doing the same job.
To be told you are not enough.
To have your stomach bloat up when your ovaries are at
work.
To have saggy boobs.
To wrap them around with tape because they get in the way.
To have your organs removed.

Love is her

To not really know what an orgasm feels like.
To be paralyzed in bed at the hands of a man.
To weep into your pillow.
To feel unlovable.
To feel not enough for him.
To be laughed at because your ass is too big and your legs are
too long.
To be told you are too fat.
To not fit in your pants.
To loathe yourself.
To have your hair fall off.
To have it in all the wrong places.
To be stood up on a Friday night.
To have never received that call back.
To be told you love too much.
To have your bones enlarged to gestate another human life.
To sacrifice your life to be a mom.
To make another choice.
To feel incomplete because your eggs don't work.
To birth a dead baby.
To lose your child in a crowd.

To sit in front of the bus for the first time.
To protect your children with your claws.
To have your kids' tears running down your shoulder.
To be called a mother, and a sister, and a daughter.
To know freedom is what it looks like to you and not what they
have told you it is.
To fall in love with another woman.
To melt after a kiss.
To have the door opened for you.
To open your legs willingly.

To be penetrated as if he wanted to shoot stars through your
eyes.
To get your pussy licked.
To bleed.
To stain the white satin sheets.
To choose you.
To be a CEO.
To wear a red pair of very high heels.
To love yourself crazy.
To feel ancestral pain chilling your blood.
To have every other woman's genetical memory tattooed on
your brain.
To heal and feel you are healing for every other woman.
To stand up for yourself and break the oppressive patterns for
every other woman.
To be 100% you.
To be a Woman.

Our shimmering beauty is the healed scar of our suffering.
Our glow is the metamorphosis of our pain into resilience
and strength.
It's the force that pushes our shoulders back and gives us
that extra 5" of height when walking barefoot.
It's the fluorescent light against the darkness of a pitch-
black jungle.
It's an imaginary red lipstick.

What didn't kill you not only made you stronger; it made
you even more beautiful.

You learned to survive underwater and on earth.
You are naturally amphibious.

Beauty emanates from your being from the respect and
love you learned to have for yourself.
You own it, like wearing a black fitted jacket, and it
protects you.
It's venom hugging your legs like black fishnets.
If predators bite you, they are dead.

Beauty is a song.
You sing it when it rains and storms, just like a frog does.
You add dimension to the ecosystem with your voice.
You are beauty.

Love is kambo

Don't ever wish to be prettier —don't elbow the devil.
Rise in love with yourself, every day a little bit more.
Self-love is your shield, and knowing that makes you,
astonishing beautiful.

In moments of total ecstasy, I find myself saying "Fuck me!" or "Yes!" Or "Oh mygoodness!"
My voice turns deep. It has a strength to it.
I picture a redwood-tree size digging truck scooping tons of dirt across acres.
That's the strength of my cry.

But what am I really saying?

To find my answer, I dug into the depths of my soul.
I went to the center of the world that resides in my heart.

And I asked.

My heart said

You are celebrating your opening up.
You are having an opengasm.

An opengasm is a portal of exploration to your untouched self, to that true you that resides underneath the piles of dirt you have accumulated over the years.

It's the liberation of your bare soul. It's waking up from a living death. It's breaking out of the casket prison we sleep in. it's defying the behavioral protocol. It's screaming so loud we upset the neighbors. It's being brave enough to speak up for yourself and have your voice resonate in another soul. It's living up to your mission. It's not giving a fuck about what they'd say.

It's curling up on the shower floor, hugging your own torso, closing your eyes, letting warm tears run over your chest and realizing how much you love yourself–and how long you have denied meeting your own goodness. It's feeling like saying "I'm sorry"--but that's not allowed. You are sorry to have missed it for all this time, but no need to apologize. Be thankful instead. Say thank you. Kiss your knees, and your shoulders, and your hands. Hug tightly. Squeeze the living hell out of you. Thank your goodness because now you are here, opened, awakened. Liberated like a Niagara fall where *goodness* breaks out of you uncontrollably, like blood shooting out of a jugular vein.

See this strength. Believe in this intensity. Absorb it.
This is the real you.

Every time you are caught in a moment of extreme bliss –- this is what you are shouting. This is what you are craving with the strength of a 109,000-horsepower engine.

You are having an opengasm; you are opening the fuck up.

Don't weigh yourself.
Don't qualify yourself by numbers.
Your are not sold by the pound.
Wear every single pore, scar, curve, hair on your body like
you own it.
None of them have a label or a curriculum to be judged by.
For there's no one else you can compare yourself to.
No magazine, no statistic, no new lab-discovery can talk
about your body.
Your body is the suit that gloves the energy and immensity
of your heart.
Tell me, Woman, how in the world can you put a price on
that?

Love is your body

I'm late.
The positive 10th test.
Decision making.
New reality.
Hips enlarged.
Hormonal changes.
The hospital?
I need a midwife.
The 1st month.
The monthly blood tests.
The insatiable hunger.
Morning sickness.
Vomit taste.
The 3rd month.
Clothes don't fit.
The mini tummy.
The 8 pm going to bed.
The red wine cravings.
Grossed out by ice cream.
The 5th month.
The alien movements that appeared on my belly.
The glow.
The angelical sex.
The 7th Month.
The belly drops.
No more high heels.
The penguin stroll.
The lower back pain.
The wanna-stay-at-home, but still going to work.
The 8th month.
The big belly. A football? No, a basketball.
The gender guessing—All of you were wrong.

Love is the process

No memory of a flat stomach anymore.
The "OMG I'm pregnant" moment.
The sympathy pregnancy symptoms on him.
His tears. The love.
The 9th month.
Where did time go?
The cramps... Those were contractions?
The 39th week.
The day the water broke.
The damned contractions.
Legs feeling chopped off by a chainsaw,
The body starts to shiver, the back cannot support my weight --
It's getting stabbed and it's going to break.
The uterus, the stomach, heavy like a sack of stones.
Gravity is the enemy.
The adrenaline.
The cortisol.
The birth at home.
The pain, the agony again.
A contraction every 30 min? No, every 10.
Jump into the pool.
The water, my ally.
My territory.
The feline dance, I walk on all fours.
My breathing, my drug.
My eyes always closed.
My trance.
My purple heavens.

My instincts, my animal instincts.
My body and the contractions.
The contractions!... Just bringing me closer to her.
She's finally home.

Real fruits have seeds.
Just like real women have curves.
If a woman lacks curves,
it's like a fruit that has been played with,
that has been manipulated.
The juice is still there, but there's something missing.
A fruit without seeds can't produce another tree.
A woman without curves is the saddest thing I have seen
It's a woman that has been silenced.
Just like a tree that has been neutered,
whose seeds have been discarded.
Don't mess with a woman's curves.
Let beauty blossom in its course.
Let women spread their seed.
Let nature be.

Love is to blossom

I am a woman as you have dreamed of one.
I wear a sealskin and swim in the depths of the oceans.
I can breathe air for just so long but inevitably have to get
back to the salt waters.
I trace a circle on the earth around me and instantly
protect myself from the harm of ignorance.
I use my smell sense to find the cure for your aching heart
in the forest.
I'm a swan among ducks.
I talk to the trees, and they sing back to me.
I howl to bones and dirt and sticks, and life is resurrected.
I carry dolls in my pockets that help me discern good
from bad.
I'll kill if I have to.
I can give myself an orgasm just by laughing.
I play with my temple.
I'm feral.
I am from every particle of sand,
from every star,
from every drop of rain.
I am all that scares you.
I'm not from here.
I'm of the moon.
I'm feminine force.
I'm creation.

—

Ode to "Women who Run with the Wolves"

Love is a Wild Woman

Moon.
13 Phases.
Waves.
The tides.
The water.
Feminine Beauty.

Blood.
13 Phases.
Curves.
The moods.
The body.
Feminine Awareness.

Love is of the moon

She surrendered to the unknown.
She recognized she had the tools,
the knowledge and the *ovarios*
to swim through the unpredictable,
the uncontrollable
and the foggy views.
She, and every other Wild Woman.

Love is the unknown

SACRED SURRENDER

Spirituality is the preventive medicine of the soul.

Nothing is what it seems.
A sunrise is not the sun ascending through the sky.
It is the Earth rotating toward the East.
The North Star is not one star.
It is two stars positioned so closely together they shine
as one.
Things are not what they seem.

Darkness might appear as torture.
As a blinding force that hinders our souls.
But nothing is what it seems.

Darkness is but a container that magnifies the pain of
humanity,
materializing it at an individual level through our own
story.

Those suffering are not victims.
They are the warriors of the world.
The alchemists transforming their pain into gold to
teach us,
to show us that nothing is what it seems.

The least of my favorite feelings is to feel nothing.
I'd prefer so much better to feel anger, to feel pain, to feel
something.
At least I'd have strength to push the rivers out of my eyes
as if a dam had broken.
I want that fury.
I'd weep until all the anger was gone, until I had evacuated
every particle of salt from my body,
until I scrub clean from the inside,
until I feel light again.

That is my favorite feeling: the lightness of being.

Love is to feel

Mistakes. The only shade of black that torments me.
Mistakes. They materialize as a heavy black cloud over my
chest.
It presses down so hard it leaves me without breath,
without energy, without motivation to take one more breath.

But god is in everything.
In the beauty of a pine tree-covered mountain that leaves
me breathless.
In my daughter's giggles and her choking hug full of
sweetness and "I love yous," which also leave me without
breath.

If I know how to breathe after love, after being awestruck
by nature,
why can't I breathe after a mistake?

I just need one more breath.
One deep breath in, and one long, deep breath out to
forgive myself.
Forgive not for the mistake…
To understand myself for not seeing the mistake as a
teaching vehicle,
and a vessel for growth, as my friend, as god himself.

I just need one more deep breath.
To love this shade of black, this heavy and beautiful cloud
on my chest that was simply pointing out that, in life, a
choking moment of happiness or sadness requires the same
thing: one more breath.

My thoughts are not what they seem.
I am not what I see.
Here we are, both you and me,
looking at the world that is not what it seems.
It's incomplete.
Our view is incomplete if we can't see what can't be seen.

The text that wasn't sent.
The "I love you" that wasn't said.
The tears hiding behind our eyes.
The fear dressed in camouflage.
The longing.
The innocence.
The spirit.
These are the things that can't be seen, the ones that
complete the truth of who we are.

We are not what we see.
Next time you are in a quarrel, next time you are pissed
off, next time he or she hurts you, look past what you see
to find what they don't want you to see.

You'll be able to see your whole world in them reflected
back to you.

If I had the chance to grant you something, I'd wish to give you the miraculous force of forgiveness.

I so wish it was a thing like a bag of gold coins, or a ginger spiced candle.
The candle would work like a switch, and when it was done burning, you'd heal, and you'd forgive yourself.

I so wish you could see yourself with my eyes.
It will blow you away how much light emanates from your heart.

I so wish I could give you a bit of my strength and you could wear it like a biker jacket. And you would just walk around painting the town red, in your cool, knowing that everything is always okay.

But I can't. I can't grant you these things.
They are not things but truths that reside within you.
Only thing is, you have chosen to neglect them.

You hate with conviction aspects of you.
I love with my all, all of you.

May our path be one of forgiveness, one of healing and understanding, so we can inspire others who hate with conviction to forgive themselves and love themselves unconditionally with that same audacity.

Love is your truth

The ultimate testament of self-love is finding grace even as you are falling into quicksand.

Finding grace is finding the beauty during the compressing, suffocating moments when your heart is off beat, your thoughts repeat like a scratched record, and your hormones are having a ball.

Finding grace is, in spite of it all, holding your own hand, having your own back, and walking yourself home.

Finding grace is replacing self-judgement with self-observation.

Finding grace is staring at your eyes and reminding yourself that the biggest success of your entire life is being alive, right here, right now.

To love yourself is the most gracious waltz there is.

Life is so fragile.

The heart can stop beating at any second, and we can't argue with it if it does.

And yet, we wake up sometimes dreading to get out of bed because the responsibilities are too many, or because work is awful, or because we can't simply understand the simplicity of being alive—of a heart that keeps beating.

Life is fragile.

But a force that defies gravity has elevated us from the ground.
It managed to stand up our bodies on two feet, got our shoulders back, head high, and heart beating.

These bodies are filled with a life force that keeps the heart pumping.
A heart whose stubborn way of staying alive, of loving life, of being kind, inspires another heart that perhaps is looking at the sky for answers.

But all answers are within that beating heart.
They are within you, not in the sky.

That heart of yours beams light to yet unreached distances.
That heart of yours makes it easier to understand, that life is simple.
That life is to be enjoyed.

Love is you

And, to all those hearts that stopped beating unexpectedly; your light was electricity-force that revived our hearts so many times; it illuminated our skies, it was the moon in our nights.

Because of you, our heart beats profusely.
You changed us, gave melody to our pulsing organ.
Because of your heart, our life is richer.

Life is so fragile.
—

To my dear friend, Christian de la Iglesia; your heart will be remembered forever.

It just occurred to me that the experience of giving birth is the same excruciating pain of letting go of something that you love.

The parent in you wants to keep the love safe, near you, close to your heart, dependent on you.

But that love has a life of its own. It has its own destiny, of which you have no control, even if you are its creator. Since the moment of its conception, that love hasn't stop growing, and it will never cease to do so.

It made a cozy home out of your body and your blood, but the time comes when you have to let it go.
To our mind, this sounds like abandonment, a lack of appreciation, but that's not the truth.

Truth is, your body is an instrument of the universe.
The life or the love that the body produces is not yours, just as a guitar can't claim the song as its own.
We are but indispensable tools for the process of love making.

We produce some amazing tunes, some beautiful relationships, but we must release them.
Just like moms have to deliver babies, we too, must let a relationship cruise its own rivers.
We must allow them to connect back to its own rhythms, and our loved ones get back to their path.
They don't belong to us.

Love is to let go

Yeah, letting go is painful, but isn't it the same thing as giving birth?
And there isn't anything more beautiful in this entire universe than being used for the manifestation of love.

Go ask your mom.

Love is not the process through which you become whole.
Love is the process through which you become
undone. Love celebrates your wholeness.
Love deconstructs your thoughts of unworthiness. Love
heals.

⟮⟯

Love is celebration

Pray. Meditate.
Send your love to loved ones and to those whom you love
with difficulty.
Pray. For when we pray, we speak to each other from our
collective consciousness.
And it's from our collective consciousness that we
download the inspiration to deal with the everyday.

Meditate. Straighten your back.
Practice how to show up in life.
Seek alignment.
Know the difference between being vertically present and
standing sleeping.
Send your love. Send your blessing and your light.
As you do, you transform your own hate, your own
judgments and frustrations with the world.

When you don't know what to do.
When you're not capable of dealing with our collective
pain.
When the world seems doomed. Or not.

Pray. Meditate. Send your love.

Love is prayer

Yesterday evening, I was swimming in the ocean and a shark swam by me.
It almost touched me with its right fin and its coarse tail as it wiggled away.
I froze. I stopped time.
I experienced what it means to have everything happen at once.
My heartbeat was so out of control there was no space between each thump.
I suited myself in fear, as if fear could protect me — as if suddenly by wearing this cloak of panic I became invisible.
I didn't think about death, not once.
I felt instead a sense of reverence of the shark's presence.
I was star-struck, to be more precise.
I felt insignificant next to him in a sort of monumental way.
The shark simply swam away.

This morning I attended a poetry reading.
Each poet caressed my arms with their lyricism.
I felt I could almost recite their poems before they spoke them — as if we knew each other from before, as if I was reading their thoughts.
I got chills and a smile adorned my face like an oversized straw hat adorns a pretty woman's head.
But suddenly, their stories triggered tears, which washed the smile away like paper wilting under rain.
I felt fear, I felt pain.
I felt anointed with their sorrow and mine.
My heart sped until it was a flat tone as they described my most intimate secrets.
As if they had seen me cry before.

Love is reverence

As if their heart cracked just like mine did after my last
relationship.
As if my pain was theirs.
As if all pain was the same and it came from the same place —
or is it?

Now, I wonder to myself — Which is more intimidating: a
shark encounter in the open water or a poet telling it like it is?

Wanting to be seen is one of the most pitiful attributes of
the human condition.
It's the cause of all suffering.
But—
Being seen is one of the most exuberant experiences of
being human.
And—
Seeing someone is one of the most graceful acts of our
humanity.

Wanting to be seen is…
To live seeking recognition, thus your happiness is
dependent.
To fill the gaps of your heart with someone else's praise
instead of cementing your heart with your own
compassion.
To justify your story with what people do or not do, thus
you are powerless.
To think the world owes you something.
Wanting to be seen is seeking love in the wrong places.

But—

Being seen…
Ignites your existence and you detonate like fireworks.
Fills your heart with reverence and gratitude.
Reinforces your purpose in waking up every morning.
Calibrates your life's GPS.
Being seen is waking to love.

And—

When you see someone...
You find the good in other people.
You love unconditionally.
You light up rooms with your presence.
You can claim yourself immortal because when you see someone,
your image will live eternally in the minds of those you've seen.

Of course, we want to be seen.
How could we not?
But be careful what you wish for.
Wanting to be seen is the mind's addiction.
See instead.
See your soul.
Recognize the ability you have to transform your life when you see yourself.
Then, you might see someone else.
And you'll light up your way to the heavens detonating sparkles in someone else's eyes.

SACRED
GOOD
BYE

I was born on January 1, a peculiar day to be born.
I'm a testament to that peculiarity, as I do nothing in my life the
ordinary way.
I've always said I'm creative out of my own rebellion.
It is in my nature to break the mold, to look under the rug, to
try the path less traveled.
That is how I find creative solutions to lead the life I want.

My life is a dance. It has spins and turns and ups and downs.
It's a seductive, sometimes painful dance.
It is the rhythm, however, that melody of impermanence, which
flavors my life.

It's the contrast that allows me to appreciate the predicaments
and pleasures of life.
The joy of one kiss or the darkness of my mind.
Swimming in the ocean or losing a friend.
It's cooking. Being a mother. Receiving a hug.
Riding a wave or a bad day.
I'm happy for my stories and for my tragic comedies.
I'm happy I was given the privilege to be alive.
I love that I feel. I love my curiosity.
I love the rebellious dancer that I am.

Thank you for reading my heart.

To be continued...

Thank you, Mama Killa

About the Book

Woman of the Moon is a poetry book that speaks to the heart in the heart's own language.

Our minds often try to label earthly occurrences, but only our heart can make sense of them. That sense is not always the explanation we want to hear but that sense fills our guts with such emotion that its answer transforms the meaning of our existence.

This book is filled with wild feminist prose proposing the liberation of the soul from the oppression imposed by a society driven by the ego mind. Pamela's poetry spills love over the pages; it is a dance between stanzas that describe the need for a radical sense of self-love, a gut-adoration for life, and a deeper look at our collective relationship with the world.

WOM celebrates life on this planet for the short period of time during which we are fortunate enough to be here. Our bodies might be from this Earth, but our souls are of the Moon.

Printed in the United States
By Bookmasters